WORDS FOR
SPEECHLESS MOMENTS

Guidance, Stories and Jokes
for
Speeches on all Occasions

'Edison said – "Genius is 1% inspiration and 99% perspiration". Composing and delivering this speech can also be described in percentage terms. The 1% inspiration may be there, and certainly no more in my case. There is about 40% perspiration, little of which can, I hope, be detected from where you are sitting. Another 40% is sheer desperation and the fact that I got on my feet at all relies on the remaining 19% being advanced inebriation.'

The Author

WORDS FOR SPEECHLESS MOMENTS

Guidance, Stories and Jokes for Speeches on all Occasions

by Don Foreman

Illustrations by Tim Catchpole

LONDON NEW YORK SYDNEY TORONTO

This edition published 1995 by
BCA by arrangement with
Spellmount publishers

CN 8445

Copyright © Don Foreman 1995
Illustrations © Tim Catchpole

First published in the UK in 1995 by
Spellmount Limited
The Old Rectory
Staplehurst
Kent TN12 0AZ

The right of Don Foreman to be identified
as the author of this work has been asserted by him
in accordance with the Copyright, Designs
and Patents Act 1988

Typeset by SX Composing Ltd, Rayleigh, Essex
Printed in Great Britain by Mackays of Chatham plc

ACKNOWLEDGEMENTS

I would like to thank my publisher, Jamie Wilson, and contributors Joe Starling, Robert Hardcastle, Ian Morley-Clarke and the many friends who have shared their favourite stories with me.

CONTENTS

INTRODUCTION

For many people the thought of having to speak in public strikes fear into their hearts. But it does not need to be an ordeal, and can be the happy experience it ought to be. This little book sets out to give a few hints which might be useful to anyone called on to make a speech and, as most speeches are meant to be entertaining and humorous, the jokes which follow could be useful, too! You can adapt them for the occasion at which you will be speaking, and will probably find one or two which have a relevance to the chief guest.

Public speaking really is not that difficult. Most of us speak to someone else every day, and there can be very few among us who have never told a joke and made someone laugh, or talked of a particular experience and kept the listener interested for at least a few minutes.

I suppose most people think the occasion at which they are most likely to have to make a speech, at some time in their lives, is at a wedding. By tradition the bride's father, the groom and his best man are all required to say something. But there are many other opportunities to address an audience, from happy family gatherings to celebrate birthdays, anniversaries and christenings, to political meetings, where such a happy family atmosphere might not prevail! Freemasons, Rotarians and members of similar societies are all called on to make speeches at some time or other, sportsmen will want to say something appropriate on receiving or presenting prizes, and at work managers often have to make at least a few remarks when giving farewell gifts to people leaving work on promotion, maternity or retirement – and the recipient will often want to say something more than just 'Thank You'.

There are times when you have to speak as a matter of duty, while on others it is very much an honour. In the former case it is expected that because of your position or circumstances you will acquit yourself creditably. In the latter you know that whoever has asked you to speak has done so because he or she thinks you will do a good job, and you will want to do your very best to live up to the faith which your relation or friend has placed in your abilities!

In either case you will find the experience more of a pleasure if you do a little work beforehand, and because you are obviously enjoying making your speech, the audience will enjoy listening to it. Most importantly, never forget that all those listening to you are 'on your side', and if they sense you are nervous will be very supportive – if only because they are glad it's you 'up there', and not them!

As with so many tasks, the secret is in the preparation. As soon as you know you have to make a speech, start to gather material. Don't leave it to the last minute, and don't rely on committing your ideas to memory, write them down straight away. If you think you are going to be asked to speak fairly often, it might even be worth keeping your own joke book in which you can record jokes you have heard, and humorous cuttings from newspapers and magazines.

For the personal touch, if the speech is to be made in honour of a particular person, do a little research and find out something about them. Ask family and friends for amusing anecdotes, and see if there is any significance in important dates in their lives. For example, I once delivered a speech as best man on a day which just happened to be the anniversary of the abolition of slavery, which gave an opportunity to joke about the groom having avoided hours chained to the kitchen sink thanks to the efforts of William Wilberforce!

There are books of sample speeches which may be useful to some people, but I think it is better, if you can, to write your own. People write as they speak, and to read someone else's speech is not easy. When I am asked to write a speech I politely decline. I will gladly supply ideas and suggest what I think is an appropriate line of approach and suggest suitable stories, but it is for the person delivering the speech to compose it themselves in their own words and style. Only once did I write a speech for someone, only to hear my best material ruined by a poor delivery. My best jokes fell flat and the phrasing which I thought was so clever became meaningless. The man delivering 'my' speech did not understand the jokes, so how could the audience?

Do not be ashamed to read from notes if it will make you feel more confident and help you to achieve a better 'performance'. I always use notes, telling my audience that I do so for two reasons. The first is to prove to them that I actually can read, and the second is that if I didn't have notes I would forget all the important things I wanted to say! Some people are able to use a small card with a few key words jotted down on it as an aide memoire, while I prefer to type my speech, and then cut it up into postcard size sections. If this is the method you wish to adopt remember to make sure your writing or typing is clear. Always read through your speech out loud a couple of times beforehand. That way, when it comes to 'the real thing' it will sound natural and you will avoid stumbling over names or words which are unfamiliar. Remember – if you are using notes don't bury your head in them, but speak over the top to your audience.

Of course, if you are one of those people who have the gift of delivering the perfect speech without any form of written assistance you are very lucky indeed. It should go without saying that speeches meant to be 'from the heart' are better delivered without notes. For example, it would look decidedly insincere if the father of the bride read from a card 'I am lucky to have a beautiful daughter'!

Don't go on too long, but if you have got something to say don't be afraid to take as long as you need to say it, assuming you have the attention of your audience. I remember that a former vicar of my church in South London came back from his new church in the North of

England to preach. His opening remarks from the pulpit were 'I suggest you make yourselves comfortable, because if you think I have driven 250 miles to deliver a five-minute sermon you are mistaken!' I used much the same form of words when I flew to Pennsylvania to act as best man for an old friend.

If possible check out where you are going to speak. It would be embarrassing to say the least to fall up a step or trip on a microphone wire on your way to the lectern. Even if you are speaking after a dinner, and if you have the chance, stand in your place before the function and try to imagine how the room will look once all the diners are seated. It is surprising how different things look when you suddenly stand up and see a sea of faces looking at you. Don't assume that everything will be ready for you. Remember what happened when The Queen responded to President Bush's address of welcome on her arrival in the United States. After he had spoken the President forgot to put in place the platform behind the lectern so when Her Majesty stepped forward to the microphone all that could be seen was a talking hat!

While you should avoid shouting, remember that in a large room a quiet, mumbling voice will not be easily heard, and the attention of the audience will wander. People may start to talk to their neighbours, the resultant noise making it even more difficult for you to be heard. An obviously uninterested audience is very unsettling for even the most experienced speaker. So, speak up, speak clearly and vary the pitch of your voice to avoid a droning monotone. In a room which is small enough for your voice to be heard do not use a microphone simply because it is there and you think it is the right thing to do. It may seem an exciting novelty to handle the mike like your favourite singer, but microphone technique is not as easy as it looks, and the effect could ruin your speech, rather than enhance it.

Having put a great deal of effort into preparing your speech, try not to hurry it, however much you might want to get it over and done with! Give the audience time to get the jokes and understand the references you are making. You know the joke already, but it may take some slower minds than yours a moment or two to cotton on, so give them time. And as any great comedian will tell you – it's the pause which can be as funny as the joke itself.

Another fault to avoid is distracting the audience with annoying gestures like fiddling with your jewellery, waving your spectacles or jingling coins in your pocket. This tendency can be overcome by holding your notes or resting your hands on the lectern, if there is one. Once you are settled you can then use your hands to make the natural gestures we all use when speaking.

Try to be aware of any expressions, cliches and words which you use frequently in normal speech. What I have in mind are the irritating 'you know', 'right', 'like' and 'I mean' which pepper some people's everyday conversation. I once worked for a director who used to begin virtually every other sentence with 'clearly'. The result was that those listening were more interested in counting the 'clearlys' than the subject of the speech in the hope they had won the sweepstake which the company secretary ran on each occasion. I once won myself, having successfully guessed there would be 27 'clearlys' in a ten minute talk.

If you are very nervous of speaking, here are two hints which might help overcome those nerves. When you get to your feet don't immediately start on the 'formal' part of your speech, but just make a conversational remark about the weather, or the traffic delays, or something quite unimportant which will let you get used to hearing your own voice in an unfamiliar situation. If you are overawed by a large audience and feel intimidated by so many pairs of eyes staring at you, just concentrate on one familiar face, your sister, husband, old school-friend, it doesn't matter who as long as it gives you the confidence of speaking to someone with whom you are used to having a one-to-one conversation. Then, once the nerves have subsided, you can let your gaze range over the audience.

I am sometimes surprised by how broad-minded people have become, so it would be pointless to issue stern warnings about avoiding smutty jokes. My own rule of thumb is that if a joke, or one very like it, has already been told on the television or radio, or printed in a newspaper, and in a programme or journal which members of your audience are likely to have seen, heard or read, you are generally safe in including it. What is important is to be aware of your audience. A story which would be well received at a rugby club dinner or a bridegroom's stag night would be highly unsuitable for a Vicarage tea party. It would obviously be tactless in the extreme to tell a joke, however innocuous, about death or illness if you knew someone in the audience had recently been bereaved or was seriously ill. Political correctness is not necessarily the force it is made out to be – my Irish friends actually ask me to tell Irish jokes – but unless you are absolutely sure of your audience it is best to avoid jokes which you think might cause offence or embarrassment. If in doubt, leave it out!

Finally – remember that while it may be useful to fortify yourself with a stiff brandy before you get up to speak, two stiff brandies may cause you to fall down again!

1

GENERAL

During the last war a Cockney lad was sent to work on a farm in the West Country, part of a nobleman's large estate. One day he was working in the yard when a splendidly turned out gentleman rode his horse up to the closed gate. 'Open the gate' he shouted. The lad worked on. 'Open the gate' shouted the rider, even louder. Still the lad worked on, taking no notice whatever. Apoplectic with rage the rider bellowed 'I'm Lord Fortescue – open this gate'. This time the lad calmly looked round and said 'I don't care if you're Lord Fiftyscue, my boss doesn't pay me to open gates for you or anybody else!'

*　　*　　*

A man opened the door to a salesman, and in answer to his question said 'No, I'm afraid the head of the household is out – I'm just the chairman of the fund-raising committee.'

*　　*　　*

A country boy was walking along a road with a piglet under each arm. On the way he saw an attractive young woman, who was obviously very upset. He asked her what was troubling her and said that as it was getting dark she was afraid to follow a footpath across the field on her own. The lad offered to accompany her, and they set off, but they had not gone far when the girl began to cry. 'What's the matter now?' he asked. 'I've just realised I don't know you, and you might molest me.' 'How can I molest you? I've got a pig under each arm!' 'Well,' she said, 'I could hold one for you.'

*   *   *

Woken up in the middle of the night by screams coming
from the neighbouring house, the wife turned to her
husband and said 'It sounds as if the woman next door is
having a fit.' 'Yes,' responded her husband, 'a tight one.'

*   *   *

Tony and Sue are the most compatible couple I know –
every Saturday night they both have a headache.

*   *   *

My wife and I still have romance in our lives. We have
candle-lit dinners twice a week. She goes on Tuesdays, I
go on Thursdays.

*   *   *

On average a man makes love twice a week, which
means that while I've been speaking to you 227 million
men around the world have been having a better time
than you have.

*   *   *

I went into a large department store and just could not
remember what I had gone there to buy. An assistant
came to help me but I had to admit I had forgotten
whether I wanted to buy a camisole or a casserole. 'That
rather depends, sir,' she said, 'on whether the bird is
alive or dead.'

*   *   *

These extracts come from letters sent to a Council's
Housing Department:

I wish to complain that my father hurt his ankle very

badly when he put his foot in the hole in his back passage.

The lavatory is blocked! This is caused by the boys next door throwing their balls on the roof.

This is to let you know there is a smell coming from the man next door.

The toilet seat is cracked. Where do I stand?

I am writing on behalf on my sink, which is running away from the wall.

I am still having trouble with smoke in my built-in drawers.

I request your permission to remove my drawers in the kitchen.

Our lavatory seat is broken in half and is now in three pieces.

Can you please tell me when our repairs are going to be done, as my wife is about to become an expectant mother.

I want some repairs doing to my cooker, as it has backfired and burnt my knob off.

The toilet is blocked and we cannot bath the children until it is cleared.

The person next door has a large erection in his back garden which is unsightly and dangerous.

Will you please send someone to mend our broken path. Yesterday my wife tripped and fell on it and now she is pregnant.

Our kitchen floor is very damp. We have two children and would like to have a third so will you please send someone to do something about it.

Will you please send a man to look at my water. It is a funny colour and not fit to drink.

Would you please send a man to repair my spout. I am an old age pensioner and need it straight away.

I awoke this morning and found my water boiling.

This is to let you know that our lavatory seat is broken and we cannot get BBC2.

*   *   *

My brother is a musician. He plays a mixture of 'country' and 'rap'. We call it 'crap'.

*   *   *

There was a young couple named Kelly,
Who were found, stuck, belly to belly,
Because, in their haste, they'd used library paste
Instead of petroleum jelly.

*   *   *

A cannibal and his son were walking through the jungle when they saw, across a clearing, a beautiful young woman. The son, who was not very bright, said to his father – 'Gosh, just look at her! Let's take her home and eat her for dinner!' His father replied 'I've got a better idea. We'll take her home and eat your mother.'

*   *   *

An intellectual is someone who can listen to the William Tell Overture without once thinking of the Lone Ranger.

*　　　*　　　*

I wouldn't say my wife is ugly, but she has just got a job as a test pilot in a broom factory.

*　　　*　　　*

If condoms were sold by size they would have to be called 'large', 'extra large' or 'jumbo', because no man would want to ask for 'small'.

*　　　*　　　*

I had hoped that Marvo the human time-bomb would be here to entertain us, but unfortunately he's gone off on holiday.

*　　　*　　　*

During the Great Depression of the 1930's Lord Curzon and a friend were walking down Bond Street, and they stopped to look in a silversmith's window. After a moment Lord Curzon pointed out a display of items and asked his friend what they were. 'They're napkin rings,' he replied. After a pause his lordship said 'And what might they be for?' 'Well, Curzon,' explained his friend, 'some people can't afford to have a clean napkin with every meal, so they roll it up after dinner, put it in the napkin ring, leave it on the table and use it again next time.' 'Good Lord,' exclaimed Curzon, 'can there be such poverty?'

*　　　*　　　*

A girl asked her boyfriend to spend the evening with her, as her parents would be out at the opera. Realising the opportunity this presented he made sure he bought the necessary items at the chemist early in the day, and arrived at her house full of expectation. He was introduced to the girl's father, who asked him if he would like to stay at the house alone with his daughter, or take her, with them, to the opera. When he chose the opera the girl was astonished and whispered to him 'You didn't tell me you were interested in opera.' 'You didn't tell me your father was a chemist,' he whispered back.

*　　*　　*

The man in front of me at the counter in a toyshop bought the two little boys with him a drum and a trumpet. 'You might regret this one day,' said the assistant, 'the noise will drive you mad.' 'No it won't,' said the man, 'they live with their mother.'

*　　*　　*

The church women's group announced a rummage sale, asking for 'All those things which you don't want to keep but are too good to throw away. Bring your husband.'

*　　*　　*

Visiting a stately home a woman asked the gardener the best time to take a cutting of a particular shrub. 'Not when I'm looking,' he advised.

*　　*　　*

After a stressful and exhausting day at work a young man boarded the 'bus for his homeward journey, and took the last seat. At the next stop a tall, slim woman got on, stood next to him and glared when he didn't give up his seat for her. As the 'bus lurched along she deliberately fell against him, and without saying anything made it quite obvious she expected him to stand, but his tiredness was greater than any feelings of chivalry he would normally have. Eventually she spoke, 'Isn't it time you gave up your seat for a pregnant woman?' Completely taken aback he responded 'I didn't know you were pregnant! How could I know when you are so slim? How long have you been pregnant?' To which she replied 'About twenty minutes – but it doesn't half make your back ache!'

*   *   *

Soon after he became Party Chairman, Leonid Brezhnev took his old mother to see his sumptuous apartment in the Kremlin. From there the two of them travelled in a sleek chauffeured limousine to his dacha in the countryside outside Moscow. Next they flew by private jet to the Crimea, and his villa on the Black Sea coast. The old lady was almost overcome by the magnificent lifestyle now enjoyed by her son, but gave him a warning – 'Leonid, Leonid, never let the Communists find out about all this or you'll be in terrible trouble!'

*   *   *

Some years ago The Queen entertained Mikhail Gorbachev to luncheon at Windsor Castle. During the meal Gorbachev was appalled to see his secretary, Feodor Pavlovich, surreptitiously secreting a gold spoon up his sleeve. Overcoming his shock at such audacity, Gorbachev thought he would also try to take a souvenir from this unique occasion.

Unfortunately luck was not with him for he dropped his spoon and managed to catch it before it hit the floor, but not before all eyes had turned towards him. Thinking quickly he blurted out: 'I will now astonish you with Russian magic. I will place this spoon in my pocket, so, while my secretary will make it appear again from his sleeve!'

*   *   *

Researching a December feature for his newspaper a Washington journalist telephoned the French Ambassador and asked him what he wanted at Christmas. Without hesitation he said 'Peace throughout the world'. He then rang the Russian Ambassador and asked the same question, receiving the answer 'Freedom from starvation, poverty and disease for people in all nations'. Next on the list was the British Ambassador who, when he was asked what he wanted at Christmas, thought for a moment and then said 'A few bottles of scotch would be rather nice'.

*   *   *

I knew my children were growing up when they realised the volume knob also turns to the left.

*   *   *

What did the 'bus conductress say to her husband on their wedding night?
   'Haven't you anything smaller? I've only just started!'

*   *   *

In the European Heaven the cooks would be French, the lovers Italian, the mechanics German and the police British, while the whole would be run by the Swiss.
   In the European Hell the cooks would be British, the lovers Swiss, the mechanics French and the police German, while the whole would be run by the Italians!

*   *   *

A woman wanting to make a soft toy went into a draper's and asked a young female assistant where she could get felt. 'Try the manager's office,' she told her.

*   *   *

On the occasion of his leaving office General de Gaulle and his wife hosted a lunch attended by the then British Prime Minister Harold Macmillan and his wife Lady Dorothy. During the course of polite conversation the

PM's wife asked Madame de Gaulle what she was looking forward to most when her husband retired. Madame replied, in a loud and clear voice – 'A penis.' Conversation abruptly stopped until the General broke the embarrassed silence by saying to his wife 'Non, cherie, in English the word is pronounced 'appiness.'

*   *   *

I don't like these wife-swapping parties when you throw your keys into the middle of the room. The only time I took part I picked out the key to the AA box on the Scunthorpe by-pass.

*   *   *

What is the difference between a man and a woman? A man can walk past a shoe shop.

*   *   *

During the course of an extremely heated debate in the House of Commons an MP shouted at a Member on the opposing side 'The Honourable Member has the manners of a pig!' The Speaker stopped proceedings, reminded the Member of the rules governing unparliamentary language and demanded that he withdrew the remark. 'I do so unreservedly,' he responded, 'the Honourable Member hasn't got the manners of a pig!'

*   *   *

When I asked one of my colleagues why he didn't take the boss home for dinner he answered 'She's already there!'

*   *   *

The British Governor of a small African colony presided over the country's independence celebrations. Almost the whole population assembled in the 'National Stadium' – a field with a large corrugated iron shed at one end – to hear the Governor in full regalia of white uniform, plumed hat and sword, make the speech transferring the reins of government to their own leaders. 'On behalf of the Great White Queen,' he began, 'I bring you greetings from the people of Britain on this historic occasion.' A cry of 'Umbala' went up from the sea of faces before him. Although he had never troubled to learn the local language he was encouraged by this response, and went on. 'While you will be independent from mid-night, you will always have a place in our hearts.' Another cry of 'Umbala', even louder, echoed across the stadium. The Governor continued. 'And we in Britain will be ever ready to help you as we have done in the past.' This sent the crowd leaping up and down yelling 'Umbala' at the top of their voices. Well satisfied with his performance the Governor handed the formal documents to the tribal chief standing with him on the podium, and who congratulated him on his speech. As a mark of special appreciation he then invited the Governor to inspect the tribe's sacred bull, but warned him 'Be careful you don't step in any of the umbala.'

* * *

A man desperate to find work noticed a newspaper advertisement for male nude models offering £50 for each published photograph. Keen to earn such a sum for no greater effort than taking off his clothes he was attracted to the idea and was disappointed when his wife disapproved. 'Do you think I would be demeaning myself?' he asked her. 'It's not that,' she replied, 'but if any of my friends saw a photograph of you in the nude they would think I'd married you for your money.'

* * *

2

ANIMALS

A security guard was so devoted to his alsatian dog that he even took it on his honeymoon. When he came back his friends asked him how it went. 'Very well except for the first night' he said. 'Why, what happened?', his friend wanted to know. 'The dog threw a bucket of cold water over us!'

*   *   *

Why is it that the new and expensive tropical fish you buy for you aquarium is always eaten by one that costs a few pence?

*   *   *

The National Canine Defence League is offering a free neutering service, aimed particularly at those on a low income.

*   *   *

A concerned couple in New Zealand broke into a car to release a dog locked inside. It turned out to be a stuffed dog put there to deter people from breaking into the car.

*   *   *

A newspaper small ad read: 'Rottweiler bitch, lovely temperament, reluctant to let go.'

*   *   *

*   *   *

A sign outside Entebbe Zoo, Uganda, states: 'Please do not feed the animals. If you have any suitable food please give it to the guard on duty.'

*   *   *

A little boy was taken to the zoo by his mother, and enjoyed it so much next day his father took him. The lad went straight to his favourite animal – the elephant. As they stood looking at the huge beast the boy asked his father 'Dad, what's that long thing hanging down from the elephant?' 'That's his trunk, son,' his father told him. 'No, Dad, I mean the thing at the other end'. 'Oh, you must mean his tail,' replied his father. 'No, the thing in between,' the boy explained. Somewhat embarrassed his father said, 'Well, what did your mother say it was?' 'She said it was nothing!' 'That's the trouble with your mother,' his dad told him, 'she's been spoiled!'

*   *   *

An ornithologist was addressing a meeting about the joys of his hobby. 'And where would we be,' he asked his audience, 'without the beautiful dawn chorus?' From the back of the hall came the shout 'Asleep!'

*   *   *

I accompanied a friend to a horse-dealer's, where she hoped to buy a pony for her daughter. The dealer brought out one old nag which puffed and wheezed its way around the yard, every step making its sides heave as it struggled for breath. When it gratefully came to a halt the dealer patted it and commented 'Ain't it got a lovely coat, lady?' 'Yes,' said my friend, 'it has, but I don't like its short pants!'

*   *   *

*　　*　　*

A zebra escaped from the zoo and found itself in a farm-yard. Seeing a hen, it asked 'What are you, and what do you do?' 'I'm a hen, and I lay eggs for the farmer's breakfast,' she replied. Off trotted the zebra until it met a cow, and asked the same question. 'I'm a cow,' she told him, 'and I give milk for the farmer's children to drink.' Just around the corner the zebra saw a bull in a pen, and asked him what he did. The bull looked up and said 'Get those pyjamas off and come in here and I'll show you!'

*　　*　　*

3

BUSINESS

What is the difference between an accountant and an actuary? An actuary is good at figures but finds accountancy too exciting.

What is the difference between an accountant and a statistician? A statistician is someone who is good at figures but doesn't have the personality of an accountant.

*   *   *

There is a belief in the part of the country I come from that a mother's first kiss can influence her baby's future life. If the child is a girl, a kiss on her feet could mean she will become a dancer, while a boy might be a successful footballer. A kiss on the hands might make a boy a boxer or skilled craftsman, while a girl could be an artist, writer or pianist. A kiss on the mouth could secure the child's future as a singer. Your chairman's mother obviously made sure he is eminently qualified to sit in the position he now occupies!

*   *   *

The local Chamber of Commerce held a dinner to honour its most successful, and very wealthy, businessman. During the speech which followed he recounted how he had arrived there many years before with only the clothes he stood up in and all his possessions in a carrier bag. As they were leaving one of the guests, hoping to emulate his success, asked him what exactly he had in the bag. 'Half a million pounds,' came the reply.

*   *   *

*　　　*　　　*

At an interview for the post of company accountant the candidate was told the firm's annual turnover and asked how much tax should be paid on it. When he replied 'How much would you like to pay?' he got the job.

*　　　*　　　*

A job advertisement stated – 'Tyre fitter required. Must be prepared to work under pressure.'

*　　　*　　　*

A woman made an appointment with her bank manager and told him she wanted to open a joint account. When he asked who with she said 'Well, someone with lots of money, of course.'

*　　　*　　　*

A man went into a bookshop and asked the assistant 'Have you got Mrs Gaskell's *Cranford*?' 'I don't know,' came the reply, 'when did she order it?'

*　　　*　　　*

My first job was as a milkman's delivery boy. We would stop at one particular house where the milkman would tell me to wait by the van while he went into Mrs Pearson's 'for a cup of tea'. Twenty minutes later he would stagger out and say 'God, I could do with a cup of tea!'

*　　　*　　　*

Once upon a time, British Rail and Japanese Railways decided to stage a boat race. Both teams practised hard to reach their peak, and on the day they were both as ready as could be. The Japanese won by a mile.

Senior BR management set up a project team to investigate the reasons for this crushing defeat and recommend appropriate action. Their conclusion: The Japanese had eight people rowing and one steering. The BR team had one person rowing and eight steering.

BR's senior management immediately hired a consultancy company to conduct a study of the team structure. Millions of pounds and several months later the consultants concluded that there were too many people steering and not enough rowing.

After careful consideration the team structure was changed to: four steering managers, one executive steering manager and one rower. A new performance incentive scheme was established to give the rower 'Empowerment and Enrichment' and make him a more productive member of the team. The following year the Japanese won by two miles.

BR laid off the rower for poor performance, sold off the oars, cancelled all capital investment in new equipment, halted development of the new high speed boat, gave High Performance Awards to the consultants and distributed the money saved among senior executives.

*   *   *

Our company secretary is a clairvoyant. She always reads the minutes of next week's meeting.

*   *   *

Do you know what it means to come home after a hard day's work to find a woman to give you love, affection and tenderness? Yes, it means you are in the wrong house!

*   *   *

From the annual report of a major conglomerate:
    'It is the intention of the company to reduce overall headcount, but at the same time widen individual responsibilities in a redesigned team.'

Or, to put it bluntly:

'We shall dump a whole lot of people and the poor bastards who are left are going to have to work a bloody sight harder.'

*   *   *

Mark Twain said that a banker is a person who lends you his umbrella when the sun is shining and wants it back the minute it rains.

*   *   *

What do you call a politician who fails to get re-elected?
A consultant.
What is a consultant?
Someone who borrows your watch to tell you what time it is – and then walks off with it.

*   *   *

4

EDUCATION

Did you heard about the Latin scholar who on his wedding night was asked to conjugate but declined?

*   *   *

Testing her pupils' grammar one day, a teacher asked 'Is LOVE a noun or a verb?' One particularly knowledgeable boy wrote 'On Friday and Saturday nights it's a verb, the rest of the time it's a noun.'

*   *   *

Pupils at an inner-city school were asked to write not more than 50 words on the harmful effects of oil on fish. One 11 year-old wrote 'When my mum opened a tin of sardines last night it was full of oil and all the sardines were dead.'

*   *   *

A child's essay on 'The Opposite Sex' included the sentence – 'I do not like the opposite sex because when I want to do anything they want to do the opposite.'

*   *   *

Some years ago the Inner London Education Authority sent a list of science laboratory safety rules to all its schools. So they could be widely understood they were in several languages, including Punjabi, Urdu, Arabic, Turkish, Bengali, Chinese and Greek. Unfortunately English was not among them. As one head teacher said

'Luckily I happen to have a teacher here who is fluent in Greek who translated it for us. Otherwise we would never have known what this communication was about.'

*   *   *

An 'old boy' of a minor public school went on to achieve great success, and wealth, as an ophthalmic surgeon. After retiring, and realising that the time had come to make plans for his demise, he returned to his old school to discuss with the headmaster what gift he could give it in gratitude for his education. As they walked around the school they entered the library, where he had studied for so many fruitful hours, and decided that a stained glass window there would be an attractive and lasting memorial. The design, including a large eye, signifying his chosen profession, was duly drawn up and approved, and the necessary provision made in his will. After his death the window was put in place, and was a matter of great pride to the school. Showing it off to a group of visiting parents the head drew attention to the large eye, indicating the donor's medical specialism. One man was heard to whisper to his wife 'Damn good job he wasn't a gynaecologist'.

*   *   *

My daughter was very nervous about her first day at school, and I patiently explained that every little boy and girl has to go to school until they were sixteen. 'But mummy,' she said, 'what happens if you forget to come and get me when I'm sixteen?'

*   *   *

Those who can, do. Those who can't, teach. Those who can't teach become educationalists.

*   *   *

*   *   *

When asked by his teacher to write a passage illustrating the meaning of the word 'panic', one boy wrote – 'I've got two older sisters at home, and at the end of each month there has to be two ticks on the calendar. Last month there was only one. Talk about a panic!'

*   *   *

A small boy came home from school and told his father that his teacher didn't know what a horse looked like – because when he had drawn one she asked him what on earth it was supposed to be.

*   *   *

Here are some letters of excuse written to schools:

'I am sorry Pauline was late for school today. She was at the stop as usual at 8.30 to catch the bus but had to come back home to use the toilet and missed it.'

'Apologies for Sharon's absence from school yesterday. This was because of the nasty chaps between her legs'.

'My son has been unable to attend school as he has had bad diarrhoea through a hole in his shoe.'

*   *   *

5

FOOD AND DRINK

An elderly man walked into a pub and said to the barmaid 'Do you know, it's thirty years since I came into this pub.' 'Well,' she said, 'I'm serving as fast as I can!'

* * *

A recipe from South Africa reads:
                    Hippopotamus Stew
Cut one medium hippopotamus into bite-sized pieces. Cover with brown gravy and cook for 3 weeks at 465©F.
   This serves 3200 people. If more is needed, add two rabbits.
   For vegetarians leave out the hippopotamus and rabbits.

* * *

A note at the bottom of a steak-house menu made the following suggestion:
   'Round off your meal with a glass of port, a brandy or a Cointreau. Or, if you fancy something more exotic, just ask your waitress.'

* * *

Another restaurant menu stated: 'For dessert there is creme de menthe or raspberry pavlova or cheese with celery and gropes.'

* * *

*   *   *

A sign in a butcher's window announced: 'Eat our home-made pies, you'll never get better.'

*   *   *

The brochure of a hotel (presumably not a temperance establishment) helpfully advised guests: 'When the restaurant is closed the night porter serves sandwiches, and drinks.'

*   *   *

An advertisement for the Anjama Indian take-away in Southampton tried to attract custom with: 'Once you try our Northern curries, you will never want to try any other curries again.'

*   *   *

A man went into a pub and said to the barmaid 'Give me a pint, a pie, and a kind word.' She put the glass of beer and a pork pie on the bar in front of him, took his money and walked off. 'Hey, what about the kind word?' he called after her. 'Oh, yes,' she said, turning round, 'don't eat the pie.'

*   *   *

Wanting a packet of cigarettes a man went into a Chinese restaurant, asked for twenty No. 6, and came out with a wheelbarrow load of rice.

*   *   *

A friend is an enthusiastic home wine-maker. She invited a neighbour in to try her latest bottling, which she proudly announced had been made from rose petals gathered in her own garden. Taking a sip, the neighbour commented 'Yes, it tastes like "Peace".'

*   *   *

A new drink has come on to the market, a mixture of vodka and carrot juice, so now you can get drunk and see in the dark at the same time!

*   *   *

A man spending a night in a hotel decided to have dinner in the restaurant. On checking out next day, as well as the basic room price, he was astonished to be presented with a further bill for £2932.10. Not having the slightest recollection of how he had run up such an enormous bill he asked for it to be itemised, and it went something like this:

1 newspaper 60p
1 gin and tonic 1.50
Dinner in restaurant 20.00
3 bottles Chateau Latour 75.00
8 cognacs for hen party on next table 25.00
Sending out for 9 vindaloos 72.00
Replacing the table you were dancing on 148.00
6 bottles of Bollinger for yourself and hen party 90.00
Taking up, cleaning and relaying the restaurant carpet
                                    after you were unwell 750.00
Buying a new blouse and brassiere for the manageress
                            50.00
Private hospital treatment for the manager's re-arranged
                            features 200.00
Buying off the Chief Constable 1500.00

*   *   *

At a dinner in Zimbabwe an inexperienced waiter was told by the host not to bring the food from the kitchen into the dining-room, but to use the serving hatch. Minutes later the hatch flew open and the waiter's trousered leg appeared through the opening while he gamely attempted to climb through with two bowls of soup.

*   *   *

Gentle Jesus, all divine,
Who turned the water into wine,
Forgive us now, poor sinful men,
About to turn it back again!

*   *   *

A report in the Shropshire and Shrewsbury Examiner gave the prize-winners, and judges' comments, for wine-making in the Oswestry Women's Institute Show.

First – Mrs Collins   Fruity and full-bodied
Second – Miss Reynolds   Well rounded, with a big nose
Third – Mrs Prothero   Slightly acid, but will improve if laid down.

*   *   *

6

HOLIDAYS

Remember – if you look like your passport photograph you're probably too ill to travel.

*   *   *

An American tourist in Rome, anxious to make conversation with the locals, asked three Italian women who from history they would choose to be. The first decided on Gina Lollobrigida and when asked why replied 'What a woman, what a figure – and so many lovers!'

The tourist accepted the validity of her choice and turned to the second woman. She chose Sophia Loren, saying 'What a beautiful body, what sexy expressions she has – and as many men in her life as she wants.'

The third woman, without the slightest hesitation, said she would like to be 'Virginia Pipellini'. Neither the tourist nor the other two women had heard of Virginia Pipellini, so she was asked to tell them about her. But way of explanation she produced a faded American newspaper cutting which proclaimed 'Virginia pipeline laid by 3000 men in two days!'

*   *   *

This sign appeared in a travel agent's window – 'This month's special offer is a week in Venice for £200, including car hire'.

*   *   *

*　　　*　　　*

A pools winner from the North of England spent some of
his new found wealth on the holiday of a lifetime – a
Pacific cruise. Unfortunately disaster struck in the form of
a typhoon and the ship was wrecked. Somehow he
managed to struggle ashore, exhausted and alone, on to
a desert island.

Next morning he woke, less tired but feeling the pangs
of hunger and thirst, to find a beautiful dusky maiden,
clad only in a grass skirt, standing beside him. As he
raised himself on to one elbow she said 'I saw what
happened. You must be thirsty, put your hand up my
skirt'. He did, and there was a glass of best bitter, which
he drank greedily. When he had drained the glass she
said 'Now you would like something to eat' and again
invited him to put his hand up her skirt. This time he
found a plate of steak and kidney pudding, carrots, peas
and potatoes. As he ate he felt strength returning to his
body. The maiden then lay down beside him and
whispered in his ear 'Now you feel better, perhaps you
would like a little fun?' 'By gum,' he said, 'don't tell me
you've got a dartboard up there as well!'

*　　　*　　　*

The Australian Jumbo Jet was approaching Sydney after a
long, non-stop flight from Singapore. The pilot landed
safely and said to his co-pilot, not realising that he had
left open the passenger address microphone, 'Glad that's
over, all I want now is a warm Sheila and a cool beer!'
The Senior Cabin Stewardess rushed up the aisle to tell
him to switch off his mike, when a passenger called after
her 'Don't forget the cool beer!'

*　　　*　　　*

A travel correspondent wrote: 'At this 5 star hotel on
Spain's Mediterranean coast I enjoyed the finest cuisine

that country has to offer, the superb accommodation one would expect in a de luxe hotel, plus free golf and riding on the 750 hectare estate, all at a cost of £300 a week. For just £60 more I could have stayed in the royal suite, sleeping in the same bed as King Juan Carlos.'

*   *   *

It was reported that a tourist was lost in the mountain ranges of South Island, New Zealand, for six days without food – except for a few prunes which kept her going until she was rescued.

*   *   *

An English lady, while visiting Switzerland, was looking for a room and asked the village schoolmaster if he could recommend any. He took her to see several rooms and when everything was settled the lady returned to her home to make final preparations for her stay. When she arrived home the thought suddenly occurred to her that she had not seen a WC in the house. She immediately wrote a note to the schoolmaster, asking him where it was. The schoolmaster was a poor student of English, so he asked the parish priest for help. Together they tried to discover the meaning of 'WC' and came to the conclusion that it must be 'Wayside Chapel'. The schoolmaster then wrote the following reply to the English lady.

Dear Madam,
I take great pleasure in informing you that the WC is situated only nine miles from the house, in the centre of a beautiful grove of pine trees surrounded by lovely grounds. It is capable of holding 200 people and it is open on Sundays and Thursdays only. As there are a great number of people expected during the summer months I would suggest you come early, although there is plenty of standing room. This is an unfortunate situation, particularly if you are in the habit of going regularly.

You will, no doubt, be glad to hear that a good number bring their lunch and make a day of it, while others who can afford to go by car arrive just in time. I would especially recommend your ladyship to go on Thursday when there is an organ accompaniment. The acoustics are excellent and even the most delicate sounds can be heard everywhere. A bazaar is to be held to provide plush seats for all, since the people feel that it is a long-felt need. My wife is rather delicate so she cannot attend regularly. It is almost a year since she went last. Naturally it pains her very much not to be able to go more often.

I shall be delighted to reserve the best seat for you, if you wish, where you will be seen by all.

Hoping to have been of some service to you, I remain,

The schoolmaster

*　　　*　　　*

A notice in rooms at the Hotel New Otani, Singapore, extends the following invitation: 'Please present this card for a complimentary welcome punch in the Cinnabar Lounge'.

*　　　*　　　*

A couple's marriage was not working out too well and they decided to take separate holidays. The husband went to Torquay, and sent a postcard to his wife who had gone to the South of France. It read 'Having a wonderful time, the hotel is superb, the weather is fine and I've found a beautiful 18 year-old girl to have fun with'. She sent a card from St Tropez saying 'I'm having a wonderful time, too, I've met a handsome 18 year-old boy, and have you noticed how 18 goes into 52 more times than 52 goes into 18?'

*　　　*　　　*

*   *   *

An Englishman on holiday in France had taken lessons in French but was nervous of trying out his competence. One morning, at breakfast in his hotel, he shared a table with a French guest. Seeing a fly buzzing round he seized the opportunity to practise his French, pointed to the fly and said 'Monsieur, regardez le mouche!' The Frenchman, like most of his countrymen, was very precise about the niceties of his native tongue and corrected the Englishman. 'Non, Monsieur – la mouche'. 'Mon Dieu,' said the Englishman, 'Quelle vision exceptionelle!'

*   *   *

A British tourist on his first day in New York was approached by a guy who asked 'Excuse me, do you know where Central Park is?' When the tourist told him he didn't, the guy said 'Well, do you mind if I mug you here?'

*   *   *

7

MEDICAL

A sign on the maternity ward wall read 'The first three minutes of life are the most critical.' Underneath someone had written 'The last three are pretty dangerous, too!'

*   *   *

Some years ago an outbreak of psittacosis, the disease spread by parrots, received considerable publicity in the Press. This prompted a young woman who was feeling a bit under the weather to imagine she was suffering from the disease and sent her rushing to her doctor for a thorough examination. After the examination he was able to assure her he could find no trace of psittacosis. 'It was silly of me even to have thought it,' said the woman, 'for I've never been in contact with a parrot.' 'Maybe not,' the doctor commented, 'but I see you've had a cockatoo.'

*   *   *

A woman went to her doctor complaining of pains across her chest and down her left arm. The doctor was concerned, and asked her to strip so he could examine her thoroughly. The examination completed he said 'Well, I have to tell you you have acute angina.' 'Never mind the compliments,' she snapped, 'what's wrong with me?'

*   *   *

*   *   *

A notice pinned to the door of a family planning clinic on the Seychelles announced 'Closed for the Feast of the Immaculate Conception.'

*   *   *

My favourite magazine is 'The Lancet'. I buy it for the 'Spot the Boil' competition.

*   *   *

While on holiday in Italy I met a consultant surgeon. In the course of conversation he told me about his many trips abroad to attend conferences and seminars in exotic locations like Hong Kong, Rio de Janeiro and Singapore. Surprised he could be out of the country for so long and so often I asked him who did his work when he was away. 'The same people who do it when I'm there, of course,' he replied.

*   *   *

Peter and Edward, both doctors and old friends, met after the passage of several years. Naturally the conversation got on to the subject of health, and Peter said he was suffering from serious headaches. Edward said he had suffered, too, but his headaches were always relieved by placing his head between his wife's breasts. Peter wondered if such a remedy would work for him, and Edward encouraged him to give it a try. They met again some days later, and Edward asked his friend if his headaches were better. 'Yes, much better, thanks,' he replied, 'And haven't you got a nice house!'

*   *   *

*　　*　　*

I had to go to the doctor's last week and in front of me were three women, each accompanied by girls whom I took to be their daughters. The doctor shouted out 'next', and the first woman went in to the consulting room. As the door didn't close properly I could hear their conversation.

'What's wrong with you?'

'Doctor, I'm so depressed.'

'You're not depressed, it's just your addiction to drink. You even called your daughter "Sherry". Now go home, stop drinking and you'll be much better.'

She left and he called the next woman.

From what I could heard she had the same complaint.

'Doctor, I suffering from dreadful depression.'

'Oh no you're not. I've told you before it's your obsession with money that makes you ill. You even called your daughter "Penny". Just go away and stop wasting my time. Your health is perfect.'

With that the third woman took her daughter by the hand and said 'Come on, Fanny, we're not staying here to be insulted!'

*　　*　　*

A student nurse left the following note before going off duty:

'Mrs. Smith is due for her injection today. By today I mean tomorrow as I wrote this yesterday'.

*　　*　　*

An Irishman went to his doctor complaining of feeling generally unwell, and was given a complete examination. Afterwards the doctor told him 'Well, Mr. O'Reilly, I can't find anything physically wrong with you – it must be the drink.' 'That's alright,' responded Mr. O'Reilly, 'I'll come back when you're sober!'

*　　*　　*

*   *   *

I was walking along one day when a man rushed up to me shouting 'Call me a doctor – call me a doctor!' 'Whatever is the matter,' I said, 'are you ill?' 'No,' he replied, 'I've just passed my medical exams!'

*   *   *

Most wives suffer from sinus problems. They go to their husbands and say 'Sign us a cheque for this dress; sign us a cheque for this hat.'

*   *   *

Some weeks ago I lent a friend £10,000 for a face-lift. It was so successful now I can't find him to get my money back.

*   *   *

Amputation: An admission of defeat by surgical means.

Anaesthesia: A technique by which a state of unconsciousness and insensibility to pain are induced, enabling surgeons to work without fear of interruption.

Antidote: A substance which may be used to neutralise a poison or to counteract its effects. If you have been eating creosote, for example, you would be well advised to take a strong dose of Epsom Salts as quickly as possible, suppressing any misgivings you may have about the cure being worse than the disease.

Editor's note: We cannot imagine why anyone would wish to eat creosote in the first place but, as the fish-finger said to the processed pea, 'There's no accounting for taste'.

Autopsy: A comprehensive medical examination carried out when it's too late: cases of recovery are extremely rare.

Barium Meal: A highly photogenic liquid which is as difficult to ingest as it is to eliminate.

Moral: Never ask a radiologist for a drink.

Debtor's Palsy: A psychosomatic condition which presents as a complete paralysis of the thumb and forefinger of the writing hand whenever bills are due for payment. Temporary relief may be obtained by the use of a plastic credit card, but the only permanent cure is a massive injection of funds.

Dermatology: Many disorders of the skin clear up of their own accord: a most satisfactory state of affairs for those responsible for diagnosis and treatment. Even the more persistent, unmanageable conditions do not involve sudden emergency calls, and rarely prove fatal. It follows that dermatology is a speciality to be highly recommended to young medical students.

Induction: A gynaecological procedure which has brought considerable benefit to many, as it reduces the number of duty staff required at week-ends and on statutory public holidays.

Nurses: The torch-bearers of medicine who are often told that their selfless dedication to duty reflects the greatest possible credit on the profession as a whole.
　　In other words, they do all the work while the doctors take all the credit.

Preliminary Examination: An initial procedure carried out, in the United Kingdom, to establish the general state of health of the patient and, in the USA, of his credit rating.

Pre-Med: A further check to confirm the mistakes made during the preliminary examination (see above).

Psychiatrist: A sex maniac who has failed his practical.

Rumbling (Abdominal):

> I went to the Duchess for tea,
> It was just as I knew it would be,
> Her rumblings abdominal
> Were something phenomenal,
> And everyone thought it was me.

> Editor's note: If the author of this admirable limerick would care to call at the publisher's office during normal office hours, we would be delighted to make due recognition and acknowledgement provided, of course, he is still alive. If not, we would rather he didn't.

Self-Diagnosis: A procedure involving only one idiot.

Stethoscopy: Closed-circuit eavesdropping.

Surgical Intervention: A procedure whereby you get away with grievous bodily harm, and are handsomely paid for it.

Toothache: The only known cure for overcoming the fear of visiting one's dentist. The sudden disappearance of symptoms immediately on arrival has been frequently noted but remains little understood.

*   *   *

A sign on a hypochondriac's tombstone read – 'You see! I told you I was ill!'

8

MILITARY

In 1940, when there was a shortage of serge for uniforms, a Royal Navy Fleet Order was issued stating 'Wrens' uniforms will be held up until the urgent requirements of seagoing personnel have been satisfied.'

*   *   *

A retired colonel was walking through the subway at Green Park underground station when he saw a busker playing a violin. Propped up in the violin case was a sign saying 'Please give generously – Falklands veteran'. The colonel naturally felt great sympathy for the ex-soldier who had fought for his country, and anger that he had been reduced to busking. He dropped a ten pound note into the open case and as he walked away the busker said 'Gracias, Señor'.

*   *   *

Three retired Brigadiers were chatting at a Regimental Reunion and deploring the fact that they were all getting old. 'It's my eyes that are failing', said the first. 'When I go shooting I have the greatest difficulty seeing the birds.' 'With me, it's my hearing,' said the second. 'When I play bridge I have quite a problem hearing the calls.' 'Oh, in my case it's my memory,' said the third. 'I recently hired a secretary to type my memoirs – a most attractive girl! After working late one night I took her home and suggested I might come into her flat, while she slipped into something comfortable'. She told me straight – "Brigadier – you've had it". Funny thing was – I couldn't remember whether I had or not.'

*   *   *

On the night before leaving Normandy for the Battle of Hastings in 1066, William decided to inspect his troops. The first company he visited were spearmen. He picked one at random and told him to hit a tree some 100 metres distant. The spearman hurled his spear and struck the tree fair and square. 'Well done' said the Duke and moved on to his lancers. He put a stick out in the middle of a field and selected a lancer to spike it. The young man charged across the field, spiked the stick and returned with it on his lance. 'Good show' said William and moved on to a company of bowmen. Picking out a likely lad he told him to put an arrow into a barn door about 50 metres away. The bowman loosed his arrow and off it went into the middle distance, not even hitting the barn, let alone the door. 'Watch him,' said William, 'or he'll have somebody's eye out.'

*   *   *

A private had an interview with his C.O. to ask for compassionate leave. 'You see, sir, my wife is going to have a baby.' His request was granted, and a week later the C.O. saw the private walking across the barrack square. 'Well, soldier,' asked the C.O., 'was it a boy or a girl?' 'Don't be silly, sir,' replied the private, 'it takes months!'

*   *   *

A Sergeants' Mess caterer used swill from the kitchen (estimated value £5) to feed the pig kept in the mess garden. Once it was big enough (estimated value £20) he decided to take it to market. Only £10 was offered so he returned to the base, with the pig tucked under his arm, where he met the President of the Mess Committee.

Over a drink in the bar, the president offered £15 for the pig which the caterer accepted. As the president passed over three fivers the pig seized and swallowed them. An argument followed over who was debit and who was credit. The barman acted as adjudicator and suggested that a further £15 be paid by the president. The caterer was now happy. The president was less happy, being £30 light! He decided to drown his sorrows and ordered two beers on credit, drinking one himself and feeding one to the pig. The pig burped, bringing up wind and a fiver!

At this point the Regimental Sergeant Major came into the mess and, seeing a quick way of making money, offered £50 for the pig. The president refused and ordered two more beers. After drinking his pint the pig gave another burp and another fiver. The RSM went spare, offered £100 for the pig and threatened to use his discretion regarding gaming machines in the mess. Realising he's on to a good thing the president gave the pig a third pint and was rewarded with the third fiver from the pig. The RSM offered £200 for the pig as a mess investment, which the president accepted and retired to bed.

At breakfast next morning the CO read in the local paper that his RSM had been locked up for kicking a drunken pig to death.

*   *   *

A famous General had the reputation of being a fitness fanatic, never missing his daily dozen.

On holiday in the South of France he and his wife were lying on a beach when the General announced that, on holiday or not, he was going to do twenty press-ups. 'If you're going to make an exhibition of yourself,' said his wife, 'I'm leaving right now!' – and swept off to lunch.

The general, undeterred, rolled over and started his press-up sequence. Soon after a gendarme tapped him politely on the shoulder. 'Mille pardons, monsieur,' he said, 'but madame left 5 minutes ago.'

*   *   *

*   *   *

After a heavy fall of snow the sergeant-major burst into the barrack-room and shouted 'Come on lads, hurry up and get this lot shifted before it melts!'

*   *   *

When the British Fleet under Nelson was bearing down on the French and Spanish at Trafalgar, the First Lieutenant of 'Revenge', on checking that all his men were at their proper stations, observed the unusual sight of an old salt on his knees beside his gun. 'Are you afraid?' asked the officer. 'No sir,' he replied, 'certainly not. I was just praying that the enemy shot would be distributed in the same proportion as the prize money – the greater part among the officers.'

*   *   *

Soon after women had won the right to vote a noble lady decided to stand for the constituency which is now Plymouth Drake. It was a pretty rough area and when she announced her intention to canvas votes from door to door the Commander-in-Chief Plymouth Approaches detailed a Naval Commander to accompany her, for her own safety.

On calling at one house a small girl opened the door. Seeing the lady and her distinguished naval escort she immediately invited them in. On being asked why, she replied 'Mother is out but she told me that if a lady calls with a sailor to let them use the front room and charge them ten bob!'

*   *   *

During his command of HMS Bronington, it was brought to the Prince of Wales's notice that one of the ratings was unhappy about the food served on board. The Prince, anxious for there to be no discontent among the crew, sent for the seaman and explained that there was no separate galley for officers in such a small ship. He ate exactly the same meals and found no fault with them. The rating was still not happy so the Prince told him to bring the next meal to his cabin and he would try it himself. The rating did so, the Prince tried it and found nothing wrong with it. 'Now are you satisfied?', asked the Prince. 'No, Sir, I'm afraid I would like to take this higher.' The Prince responded with 'Exactly how much higher do you think you can go?'

*　　　*　　　*

During the Gulf War British troops were visited by the Parliamentary Defence Committee. Among its members was the present Winston Churchill, MP. Approaching one platoon the MP put out his hand to a corporal, saying 'Hello, I'm Winston Churchill.' 'Oh, yes?', said the corporal, 'And I'm General Rommel!'

*　　　*　　　*

9

MOTORING

Men whose wives want to learn to drive should not stand in their way.

* * *

At the start of a driving lesson the instructor said to his pupil 'We're going out into the country today. What roadside signs might we expect to see?' After a moment's thought she replied 'Eggs for sale?'

* * *

A roadside sign at a farm entrance announced 'Potatoes'. Someone had written underneath 'Twinned with Pommes de Terre'.

* * *

Two women drivers had a collision in their cars and got out to inspect the damage. One, very upset, wailed 'My husband's a vicar, whatever will he say?' The other retorted 'My husband isn't a vicar, and I'm more worried about what *he'll* say!'

* * *

The Company Car is easily recognisable because of the special features not found in privately owned vehicles. For example:

They travel faster in all gears, especially reverse.

They accelerate at a phenomenal rate.

They enjoy a much shorter braking distance.

They have a much tighter turning circle.

They can take 'humps' at twice the speed of private cars.

Battery, water, oil and tyre pressures do not have to be checked so often.

They do not require to be garaged at night.

They can be driven for up to 100 miles with the oil warning light flashing.

They do not require reinforced suspension but can still carry extremely heavy items when moving house, taking rubbish to the tip or collecting building materials etc.

They are adapted to allow reverse gear to be engaged whilst the car is still moving forwards.

The tyre walls are designed to allow bumping into and over kerbstones.

Unusual and alarming engine noises are easily eliminated by turning up the fitted radio volume control.

Batteries are inter-changeable with private vehicles.

*　　　*　　　*

*　　*　　*

A woman came home and told her husband she had good news and bad news. He asked her for the good news. She told him 'The air-bag on the car works.'

*　　*　　*

Driving along a road one night I remarked to my passenger on the 'cat's eyes', and recounted the story of how the inventor had got the idea from seeing a cat walk towards him on an unlit road. 'Good job it was walking towards him,' he commented, 'if it was walking away he would have invented the pencil sharpener.'

*　　*　　*

10

OLD AGE

The Mayor went to an Old People's Home to congratulate one of the lady residents who was celebrating her hundredth birthday. He gave her a bunch of flowers and remarked on how well she looked. 'And why shouldn't I look well?', she snapped. 'No reason at all,' said the Mayor, 'but have you never been bed-ridden?' 'Yes I have,' she replied, 'and hearth-rugged, but I don't see what business that is of yours!'

*　　*　　*

The Accrington Observer reported the retirement of Joe Burns, who for many years had been superintendent of the municipal crematorium. He was presented with a barbecue set.

*　　*　　*

A man went to the local library and told the librarian he was interested in history and asked for a copy of 'The Joy of Sex'. When the librarian queried his choice and reminded him he had said he was interested in history he glumly admitted 'To me that is history.'

*　　*　　*

A North Wales town council proudly announced its new refuse disposal service: 'Skips will visit each neighbourhood twice a year, for a few days at a time, so that people can get rid of their bulky items. It is being particularly aimed at the elderly and infirm.'

A ninety-four year old was clearing weeds on his allotment when suddenly a frog jumped out, looked at him and said 'If you kiss me, I will turn into a beautiful princess.' The old boy picked up the frog and put it in his pocket, from where it croaked 'Why don't you kiss me? Don't you want a beautiful princess?' 'No thanks,' he said, 'at my age I'd rather have a talking frog!'

The Focus, Tunbridge Wells' free newspaper, advertised a meeting at the community centre: 'Senior Citizen's Club, illustrated talk, 2.30 pm. An exciting ride through death valley.'

The Joys Of Being Eighty

I have good news for you – the first eighty years are definitely the worst! The second, so far as my experience goes, is a succession of pardons. If you forget your neighbour's name, forget to keep an appointment, or promise to be in two or three places at one time or spell words wrongly, you just need to explain that you are eighty years old – then everyone wants to carry your bags.

At eighty you can relax with no misgivings. You have a perfect alibi for everything, absolutely everything. No-one expects much of you. If you act silly, it's your second childhood! This is a great deal better than being seventy years old or even sixty five. At that time you are expected to retire to a little house or home and become a discontented, fumbling, limping old has-been! If you survive until you are eighty, everyone is surprised that you can still walk.

At seventy people are mad at you for everything. At eighty they understand and forgive. Life really does begin at eighty! Remember too, old folk are worth a fortune – with silver in their hair, gold in their teeth, stones in their kidneys, lead in their feet and gas in their stomachs.

In have become a little older since last talking to you, and a few changes have taken place. Yes, I've become a frivolous old girl! I'm seeing four gentlemen a day. On waking up, WILL power helps me get out of bed. Then I pay a visit to JOHN. ARTHUR-ritis makes his presence felt about mid-morning. He doesn't like to stay in one place very long, so moves around and takes me from joint to joint. After such a busy day I'm really tired and ready to go to bed with VIC vapour rub. What an interesting life!

Oh yes – the vicar called the other day. He said that at my age I should be thinking about the hereafter. I told him I do, all the time. No matter where I am, in the kitchen, in the bedroom or in the shed, I ask myself 'What is it I am here after?'

*   *   *

How To Know You Are Growing Old

Everything hurts. What doesn't hurt doesn't work.

The gleam in your eye is the sun hitting your bifocals.

You feel like the morning after, but you haven't been anywhere.

Your 'Black Book' contains only names ending in 'M.D.'

You get winded playing cards.

Your children begin to look middle-aged.

You join a Health Club but don't go.

A dripping tap causes an uncontrollable urge.

You know all the answers but no-one asks the questions.

You look forward to a dull evening.

You need glasses to find your glasses.

You turn out the light for economy instead of romance.

You sit in a rocking chair and can't make it go.

Your knees buckle but your belt won't.

Your back goes out more than you do.

You sink your teeth into a steak and they stay there.

*   *   *

11

POLICE AND THE LAW

The newspaper headline read 'RARE EGGS HOARD', and the story below ran 'Police seized 1,500 rare birds' eggs from a house in Mosborough, Sheffield. A man has been questioned about a suspected poaching operation.'

* * *

The Kent and Sussex Courier printed this report:
   'Crowds flocked to the West Kent Hunt point to point races at Brookes Farm, Chiddingstone Hoath, on Saturday making it the best attended meeting since 1984. Traffic queues built up on the Penshurst to Edenbridge road with local police on traffic control. They did their job so well that a Japanese tourist on his way to Gatwick Airport was ushered into the farm and paid £10 to park before realising he had reached the wrong destination. It then took him three-quarters of an hour to obtain a refund and get back on the road.'

* * *

Four solicitors and a judge were dining together and during the course of conversation the judge, who sat at Marlborough Street Court, mentioned he had, that day, had a number of 'ladies of the night' brought before him. This prompted them to speculate on what the generic term for these women might be. In turn the solicitors suggested: a jam of tarts; a fanfare of strumpets; an anthology of prose and a novel of Trollope's. The judge listened carefully and then said 'How about a firm of solicitors?'

Police are looking for a hardened criminal following the theft of a concrete mixer.

*   *   *

A car belonging to a Jehovah's Witness was broken into and a box of books stolen. A police spokesman said 'God knows who did it.'

*   *   *

In the summing up on behalf of his client defence counsel said 'The defendant cannot be held guilty. He did not know what he was doing as at the time he was as drunk as a judge.' The presiding judge immediately interrupted and corrected the barrister. 'Surely you mean as drunk as a lord?' 'As your lordship pleases,' came the reply.

*   *   *

The police learn a lot by trial and error – usually someone else's trial and their own error.

*   *   *

A little girl walked past a police station with her father, looked up at the 'wanted' posters and asked 'Daddy, why didn't they arrest those men when they took their pictures?'

*   *   *

A 7 foot tall cardboard cut out of a policeman was stolen from outside the Council Offices – where it had been advertising a crime prevention exhibition.

*   *   *

An advertisement in 'The Times' placed by the Temple chambers of a Queen's Counsel called for 'applications from established practitioners of 5–12 years to join its busy and expanding criminal team.'

*   *   *

12

RELIGION

What was the first thing Adam said to Eve after they ate the fruit?
  'Stand back, I don't know how big this thing gets!'

*   *   *

A vicar made this announcement from the pulpit – 'We are thinking of starting a club for young mothers in the parish. If any lady would like to be a "young mother", would she please see me in the vestry after the service.'

*   *   *

Moses came down from Mount Sinai carrying the tablets of stone. The Israelites gathered at the bottom were anxious to know about the commandments God had given him. 'Well,' said the prophet, 'I've got some good news and some bad news.' 'Give us the good news,' shouted the Israelites. 'I've got him down to ten,' said Moses. 'And the bad news?' 'Adultery is still in.'

*   *   *

Adam was standing alone in the Garden of Eden when across the glade he saw a creature which looked much like himself – except for one or two details. Curious, he demanded of God, who was instantly accessible in those days, 'God, what's that?' 'Don't sound so ungrateful,' said God, 'for that is called woman, and I have made her for your own benefit.' 'Thank you very much, I'm sure,' said Adam, 'but what do I do with it?' 'Well, to start with, why don't you go over and kiss her?' suggested the

Almighty. Adam was, of course, quite ignorant of the expression 'to kiss', having led a solitary life until then, but once God had explained what to do he crossed the clearing and kissed Eve. He returned to God not very impressed, saying, 'So, is that all there is to it?' 'Oh, no,' said God, 'now you must go and caress her,' and again explained to Adam exactly what to do. This time Adam returned with a smile on his face, and eagerly demanded of God what to do next. 'You can fondle her now,' said God, and in response to Adam's request for information told him how to go about it. Within a few minutes Adam was back in a state of some excitement, saying 'come on God, what's next' for he sensed that Eve had enjoyed the fondling as much as he had, and he was anxious to please her further. 'Well, now,' said God, 'you are ready to make love to her.' 'How do I do it, how do I do it?' shouted Adam, leaping up and down with impatience. God told him and Adam rushed off across the clearing to return seconds later looking very dejected and asking the question 'God, what's a headache?'

*   *   *

One day the Vicar caught a young boy smoking. 'You're too young to smoke,' said the Vicar. 'No I'm not,' said the boy, 'I'm nearly thirteen.' 'That's dreadful,' said the Vicar, 'I'm shocked to see one so young endangering his health by smoking cigarettes.' 'That's nothing,' the boy told him, 'I had sex last night.' 'Sex at twelve years old,' said the Reverend, 'how terrible – whoever did you have sex with?' 'I don't know,' replied the boy, 'I was pissed at the time.'

*   *   *

I have a friend who is so unfit that priests send their curates round to practise giving him the last rites.

*   *   *

A young lad was left alone in the house for a while and, overcome with curiosity, took the opportunity to explore his parents' bedroom. Suddenly he heard a key turn in the front door and his mother came up the stairs accompanied by someone else who, he could tell from his voice, was a man – and not his father! There was nothing for it but to hide in the wardrobe. Through a crack in the door he saw his mother and the man kiss passionately, get undressed and climb into bed. Moments later he heard the front door open and his father call out 'It's only me – I'm home early.' His mother and the strange man leaped out of bed in panic and she bundled him and his clothes into the same wardrobe where her son was hiding. After a while the man realised that he was not alone when the lad said 'It's dark in here, isn't it?' Horror-stricken the man could only agree, and when the boy said 'If you don't give me £20 I'll tell my dad you're here', had no alternative but to pay up. Eventually they were able to escape, the man out of the window and the boy pretending he had been in his own room all the time.

Next Sunday the family was in church. When the collection plate was passed round the boy put in a five-pound note. His father was astonished and wanted to know how he had come by so much money. The boy said he had found it, but his father did not believe him and told him to go and confess his sin. As he stepped into the confessional box he said 'It's dark in here, isn't it?' and a voice from the other side of the grille groaned 'Oh, God, not you again!'

*   *   *

Mother Superior was driving with one of her nuns along a quiet road. Suddenly the Devil appeared in front of the car, forced them to stop, and threatened to deflower both of them. The terrified nun grabbed Mother Superior and wailed 'Oh, dear, whatever are we to do?' 'Show him your Cross,' said Mother Superior, so the nun wound down the window, leaned out and, shaking her fist, shouted 'Go away, you horrible creature!'

*　　　*　　　*

During the installation of new lighting in Liverpool Cathedral, one of the electricians working in the roof space accidentally left the lift door open. Nobody could summon the lift from below. Imagine the consternation of visitors when the Clerk of Works stood in the middle of the great Cathedral and yelled heavenwards 'Peter, close the gates!'

*　　　*　　　*

A vicar was leaving his parish, and at the farewell party one of the ladies of the congregation told him 'Oh, vicar, we will miss you, you've been wonderful!' 'Don't worry,' he replied, 'I expect the next will be even better.' 'I don't think so,' she said, 'that's what the last one told me.'

*　　　*　　　*

During a Communion Service the officiating priest offered a new communicant the full cup of wine with the invitation 'Drink ye all of this'. Unfortunately he did – all of it!

*　　　*　　　*

Church Announcements

Mr. Higgins has been appointed choirmaster following a stiff organ test.

On Wednesday the Ladies' Choir will meet. Mrs. Johnson will sing 'Put me in my little bed' accompanied by the Vicar.

The service will close with 'Little drops of water'. One of the ladies will start quietly and the congregation will join in.

The ladies of the church have cast off clothing of every kind and they may be seen in the basement of the church on Friday afternoon.

Trash and Treasure Sale. Ladies, look in your drawers. Your trinket may be someone else's treasure.

*   *   *

A 'Wayside Pulpit' outside a West London church announced 'If you are tired of sin – come in'. Underneath had been written 'If not – ring Hammersmith 3829'.

*   *   *

After hearing a young woman's confession, the Catholic priest, who realised she was not one of his regular congregation, asked where she was from. He was very interested when she told him that she was an acrobat with the circus then visiting the town. In fact he was so interested that he asked her, as he was too busy to see the show, to give him a demonstration of her skills. So she left the confession box and performed handstands in the aisle, somersaults, back flips with twists and all the tricks of her act. Two elderly ladies were waiting to have their confessions heard and when they saw this one turned to the other and said 'If that's what Father Murphy is giving for penance he won't be seeing me this week!'

*   *   *

The Hinckley Times reported: 'A Day of Healing with Ron Brown at Hinckley's National Spiritualist Church had to be cancelled on Saturday because Mr Brown was ill.'

*   *   *

A vicar presented prizes at the end of term Speech Day at a girls' school. After the ceremony, as he was making his way to his car, he saw the main prize-winner, an attractive, slim, blonde girl of seventeen walk past him. 'Ah, my dear,' he said, 'many congratulations. And what are you going to do when you leave school?' 'Well, Reverend,' she replied, 'I had thought of going straight home'.

*   *   *

A poster at the entrance to Hull Methodist Church welcomed worshippers with: 'Don't let worry kill you off, let the Church help'.

*   *   *

A Catholic Priest, an Anglican Vicar and a Rabbi were arguing about when Life begins. 'At the moment of conception,' said the Catholic Priest. 'At the time of birth,' said the Anglican Vicar. 'You're both wrong,' said the Rabbi, 'it's when the kids have left college and the dog has died.'

*   *   *

13

SPORT AND ENTERTAINMENT

One of the latest films to come out of Japan tells the story of the desperate plight of a wartime army unit lost in the jungles of Burma in which two officers eat their privates.

*   *   *

A radio announcer was heard to say 'We apologise for the 20 minute break in transmission during the last programme, but hope this did not spoil your enjoyment of "Thirty Minute Theatre".'

*   *   *

Here are ideas for party games. The first is called 'Twenty Questions'. Its rules are simple – you take an attractive girl into a dark and secluded place and ask her 20 questions. Of course, if the answer to the first one is 'Yes', you don't have to bother with the other 19. The second game is 'Surprises' in which everybody drinks at least a bottle of gin and the host goes out of the room. After a minute he comes back in and you try to guess who it is.

*   *   *

Sir Peter Hall was directing a play, and rehearsals were going very, very badly. In an attempt to energise the cast he told them that he was going to sit in the auditorium and they were to come on stage one by one and terrify him. They did so, in turn bellowing, screaming and shouting in a most menacing manner. Finally, Sir John Gielgud, the play's star, quietly strolled to the centre of the stage, nonchalantly took a draw from his cigarette, looked at Sir Peter, said 'We open in two weeks' and walked off.

*　　　*　　　*

An old ham actor, no longer steady on his legs and more than a trifle deaf, was thrilled when after many months with no work he landed a small part. It was only one line, but better than nothing. All he had to say, on hearing a distant offstage explosion, was 'Hark, I hear the cannons roar!' Throughout rehearsals he put all his effort into this one line, experimenting with placing the emphasis on different words. 'Hark I hear the cannons ROAR!', 'Hark I hear the CANNONS roar!' The night of the performance arrived, but when the explosion came the actor was so taken by surprise he shouted 'Good gracious, what was that?'

*　　　*　　　*

Two village cricket teams were playing their annual match when on an appeal for 'leg before wicket', the umpire gave the batsman 'out'. Walking off the pitch in a bad temper he went up to the man in a white coat and panama hat and protested that he was not 'out', adding, 'you need glasses'. 'So do you,' said the man, 'I'm selling ice-cream.'

*　　　*　　　*

Robert Morley defined football as a game in which 22 grown men kick a ball around a field for an hour and a half at the end of which time they leave it where it was and go and have a bath.

*　　　*　　　*

*   *   *

A man found himself partnering a woman at a bridge game – a woman he had never met before, let alone teamed up with at cards. She was an experienced player while he was almost a beginner, so he was rather nervous. The game progressed well enough until he came to a point when he was undecided what card to play. Looking at his partner for inspiration he noticed her hand move towards her left breast. Taking this as a signal he opted to 'pass'. They lost the game. Afterwards she asked why he had passed – hadn't he seen her signal? 'I thought I had,' he said. 'You can't have done,' she snapped, 'I put my hand on my heart and you should have laid a heart.' 'Oh, sorry,' he replied, 'I saw you touch your left tit so I left it.'

*   *   *

An old golfer, who had spent every leisure moment on his beloved game, rain and shine, realised that at his age he could be called to meet his Maker at any time. Not unnaturally he began to muse on whether there was a golf-course in Heaven, and sent up an appropriate silent prayer. To his astonishment a voice boomed back. 'I have heard your prayer and I have good news for you, but also some bad news.' The golfer asked for the good news first. 'Yes, there is a fine golf-course here in Heaven.' 'And the bad news?' 'You're teeing off tomorrow morning.'

*   *   *

A school fencing club advertised for new members with the unfortunately ambiguous invitation 'New blood always welcome'.

*   *   *

The town rifle club hoped to attract newcomers to the sport and with an eye to giving opportunities to people with handicaps announced 'We are now especially targeting the disabled.'

*   *   *

In the changing room at the squash club a man saw his friend dressing after a game in a pair of women's panties. 'Hey, what's this?', he asked, 'how long have you been wearing panties?' 'Ever since my wife found them under the back seat of the car,' replied his friend.

*   *   *

A man went into a pub and found the atmosphere completely dead. The landlord admitted that business was so bad he could be forced to close before long. Then the man noticed a piano in the bar, and suggested that if there was live music more custom might be attracted. 'That's all very well,' said the landlord, 'I've advertised for someone to play the piano but no-one is interested.' The customer then said he might be able to help as he knew someone who could play, and offered to bring him in later for a trial. The landlord, with nothing to lose, readily agreed. That afternoon the man returned, accompanied by the smallest midget ever seen. When he told the landlord that he was the piano player the landlord laughed out loud because the little fellow couldn't even climb on the piano stool. But once he had been lifted up and started to play he stopped laughing, because he was absolutely fantastic! It was arranged that the midget could stay for two days to see whether the experiment would work. Not only did it work, but it was a resounding success. The sound of happy music brought in so much trade that the landlord had to take on extra staff, and when the man returned to agree a fee for his protegee wanted to know how he had found such a talented musician. 'It's a funny story,' said the man, 'because a good fairy came to me a few days ago and offered to grant me any wish, and I don't know what went wrong, but I finished up with a twelve inch pianist.'

*   *   *

Notes